A Worthy Woman

21 Days Of Encouragement For Women

Teaira Reed

ISBN-13: 978-1981468072

You are Beautiful

You are worth Love & Affection

You are Smart

You are Kind

You are Wise

You are Unique

You are worth Happiness

You are Worthy.

-Teaira-

THE AUTHOR

Teaira Reed is an Author, Entrepreneur and Visionary Leader. She wants to keep you empowered and inspired.

Teaira Reed Books:

Empowering Your Purpose: Wisdom For Living A Fulfilling Life Of Prosperity & Purpose

A Worthy Woman: 21 Days Of Encouragement For Women

Social Media:

Facebook: @Teaira R. (Public Figure Page)

IG: @official_teairar

Email: teairalive@yahoo.com

Thank You Lord for never giving up on me when people did,

Thank You Lord for the blessings and the lessons.

Thank You Lord for every one reading this book,

Thank You Lord for giving them a NEW look on their LIFE.

Continue leading our steps and showing us the way in

JESUS NAME

-AMEN

To everyone who has purchased my books & who has supported me…

Thank You!

DAY 1

WHO ARE YOU??

You're the only one who knows the answer to this question.

Knowing yourself means knowing your strengths and weakness, your fears and passions, your desires and purpose, your likes and dislikes, your thoughts and limitations. Knowing yourself also means being in touched with your feelings and emotions. If you know who you are NOT, THEN YOU KNOW WHO YOU ARE!!! Never allow people to determine who you are. Know who you are spiritually in God. You are one of God's Creation.

Women have so many roles in life like being a mother, wife, working, nurturer, taking care of cleaning, cooking, laundry and etc. Sometimes we become lost in our roles and/or duties. Then it becomes evident that we began to feel lost and defined by our roles.

CHALLENGE In the midst of being great at what you do ...don't forget to be great at being YOU!!!

AFFIRMATION:

I AM A WORTHY WOMAN & I KNOW WHO I AM!

PRAYER

DEAR LORD,

THANK YOU FOR LOVING ME UNCONDITIONALLY AND MAKING ME WHOLE. LORD LET ME CONTINUE TO SEEK YOU AS I CONTINUE GROWING.

-AMEN-

For Ye are all children of God by faith in Christ Jesus.

-Galatians 3:26-

-SPREAD YOUR WINGS-

DAY 2

INNER SELF / OUTER SELF

Inner Conflict with yourself comes from NOT being honest with YOURSELF.

Sometimes we have false beliefs and do not believe in own true VALUE. When you are grounded in your values and preferences, you are most likely to do what you say & mean.

What do you believe about yourself?

The inner you is your spirit and it keeps right on thinking and intending. The outer you is the speaking and the acting side of you. We become frustrated when the inner self is NOT in accordance with the outer self.

CHALLENGE Evaluate your core values and remember to say what You mean and MEAN what SAY!!!

AFFIRMATION:

I AM A WOMEN OF MEANING AND VALUE!!

PRAYER

DEAR LORD,

THANK YOU FOR DOING A NEW THING IN ME. LORD, CONTINUE TO LEAD MY PATH.

-AMEN-

But he who is joined to the Lord is one spirit with Him.

-1 Corinthians 6:17-

-SPREAD YOUR WINGS-

DAY 3

HAPPINESS

Happiness is the state of being Happy.

What makes you happy?

Happiness comes when you feel satisfied and fulfilled. Happiness and enlightenment comes when you have all your needs satisfied. You will be happier when you can express who you are. Expressing your desires and preferences, will make it more likely to get the things you want. Being happy keeps you positive and full of life. Also, by being happy, we have the potential to change many other lives by being ourselves.

Your happiness is something that you deserve!

CHALLENGE Every day do something that make you feel good. Embrace the your Happy YOU!!!

AFFIRMATION:

I AM A WORTHY OF HAPPINESS.

PRAYER

DEAR LORD,

THANK YOU FOR GIVING ME LIFE AND JOY. THANK YOU FOR EVERYTHING YOU ARE DOING IN MY LIFE.

-AMEN-

FOR I KNOW THE THOUGHTS THAT I HAVE TOWARDS YOU, SAITH THE LORD, THOUGHTS OF PEACE, AND NOT OF EVIL, TO GIVE YOU AN EXPECTED END.

-Jeremiah 29:11-

-SPREAD YOUR WINGS-

DAY 4

LOVE YOURSELF

Love yourself before you try to love another. You matter first. You may desire to be loved or in love one day. How can someone truly love you, if you can't see that you are worthy of love.

Self-Love is the cure to Self-Hate. When you love yourself, you will not accept less than the love, you give YOU. Even when you feel like no one else loves you, know that God Loves you always.

CHALLENGE Look in the mirror and tell yourself .....the things you love about you!!

AFFIRMATION:

I AM IN LOVE WITH ME.

PRAYER

DEAR LORD,

THANK YOU FOR LOVING ME UNCONDITIONALLY. THANK YOU FOR YOUR GRACE AND MERCY ON MY LIFE.

-AMEN-

AND I WILL DWELL AMONG THE CHILDREN OF ISRAEL, AND WILL NOT FORSAKE MY PEOPLE ISRAEL.

-1 KINGS 6:13-

-SPREAD YOUR WINGS-

DAY 5

SELF-LOVE

NO NEGATIVE CONDITION SHALL REMAIN IN OUR LIVES.

WE SHALL EAT DIFFERENT TO REBUILD OUR BODY.

TAKE THINGS DAY BY DAY & YOU WILL BE FULFILLED.

TAKE TIME TO TAKE CARE OF YOURSELF PHYSICALLY AND MENTALLY. IT IS IMPORTANT TO LOVE YOU & BUILD VIBRANT HEALTH.

DON'T WAIT UNTIL THE THINGS WE WANT TO GO RIGHT, TO START LOVING OURSELVES. IF WE WAIT UNTIL THINGS BECOMES PERFECT WE WILL NEVER EXPERIENCE SELF-LOVE.

AFFIRMATION:

I AM WORTHY OF LOVE.

PRAYER

DEAR LORD,

I AM FOREVER THANKFUL FOR YOUR LOVE AND SENDING YOUR ONLY SON TO DIE FOR ME.

-AMEN-

FOR GOD SO LOVE THE WORLD THAT HE GAVE HIS ONLY BEGOTTEN SON, THAT WHOSOEVER BELIEVES IN HIMSHOULD NOT PERISH BUT HAVE ETERNAL LIFE.

-JOHN 3:16-

-SPREAD YOUR WINGS-

DAY 6

SELF-LOVE LETTER

DEAR READER,

LOVE YOURSELF.

LOVE THE LESSONS YOU LEARNED.

LOVE THE PERSON YOU ARE BECOMING.

LOVE THE FACT THAT YOU ARE BEAUTIFULLY FLAWED.

YOU ARE WORTHY ...... NOT WORTHLESS.

YOU ARE THE HEAD AND NOT THE TAIL.

YOU ARE ABOVE AND NOT BENEATH.

YOU ARE NOT AVERAGE.

YOU ARE UNIQUE.

YOU ARE BLESSED AND HIGHLY FAVOURED.

YOU ARE READY FOR ALL THE GOOD THINGS TO COME!!!!!

THE BEST OF YOU IS THE ... REST OF YOU!!!!

AFFIRMATION:

I AM BLESSED AND HIGHLY FAVOURED.

PRAYER

DEAR LORD,

LET ME DECREASE SO YOU CAN INCREASE IN ME. GIVE ME A PRAYING SPIRIT. LET ME WALK IN RIGHTEOUSNESS.

-AMEN-

AND I WILL DWELL AMONG THE CHILDREN OF ISRAEL, AND WILL NOT FORSAKE MY PEOPLE ISRAEL.

-1 KINGS 6:13-

-SPREAD YOUR WINGS-

DAY 7

COMMITTED TO YOU

We can become frustrated with life sometimes and give up on everything. Especially, things we been praying for. We become our own worst enemy and let ourselves down. We start to feel like destiny is so far away, when it's only so close. We get upset when people let us down. So, why is that we let ourselves down? We make promises to ourselves that we do NOT keep. We can't control people, but we can control ourselves. We can't change people, but we can change our perspective.

Don't give up on yourself.

Your vision is your Mission..... So, stay focus and keep pushing.

CHALLENGE Stay committed to the promise and the purpose. Write the vision and make it plain.

AFFIRMATION:

I WILL PROSPER AND BE GREAT.

PRAYER

DEAR LORD,

THANK YOU FOR HEARING MY CRY AND PRAYERS. THANK YOU FOR SUCCESS.

THANK YOU FOR EVERYTHING YOU HAVE SHOWN ME.

-AMEN-

"WHEN YOU GO THROUGH DEEP WATERS, I WILL BE WITH YOU."

-ISAIAH 43:2-

-SPREAD YOUR WINGS-

DAY 8

KEEP GOD FIRST

Distractions can easily throw our focus off course. That is why it is important to keep ourselves in God. Keep God first and everything will fall in place. Spending time with God, will help you see that God is in your life.

In everything you do, put God first, and he will direct you and crown your efforts with success.

If God is all you have, then you have all you need. Keep calm and know that it's in God's hand. God has a plan for you. The Lord's plan is that you prosper.

CHALLENGE Spend time with God and tell the Lord your thoughts. Spend time in prayer even if you just say … “Thank You Lord”.

AFFIRMATION:

I WILL KEEP GOD IN EVERYTHING I DO.

PRAYER

DEAR LORD,

I KEEP YOU AND MY HEART AND MIND. CONTINUE TO LET YOUR WILL BE DONE FOR ME. I TRUST YOU AND LOVE YOU.

-AMEN-

I CAN DO EVERYTHING THROUGH CHRIST WHO GIVES ME STRENGTH.

-PHILIPPIANS 4:13-

-SPREAD YOUR WINGS-

DAY 9

LET IT GO

There comes a point in our lives, that we must let go of somethings and some people. We tend to hold on to the very thing that God is trying to let go. We become so caught up on what we are losing, that we can't see we are winning. Everyone is NOT tied to your destiny. So, if people can walk out of your life.... LET THEM WALK!!! It's going to hurt letting go of people you love and care for. However, your peace of mind is priceless. Everyone can NOT go where you are going. People come into our lives to be a blessing or a lesson. You hurt yourself holding on then letting GO.

Let go of what was, for what is to COME!!! God know who's meant to be in our lives. So, if they're gone it wasn't meant for them to stay.

Some people don't serve a purpose in your life.

CHALLENGE Let Go and LET GOD!!! You deserve Peace!!!

AFFIRMATION:

I WILL LET GO AND LET GOD HAVE HIS WAY.

PRAYER

DEAR LORD,

THANK YOU FOR NEW DAYS, NEW WAYS, AND NEW THOUGHTS. LORD GIVE ME PEACE THAT PASSES ALL UNDERSTANDING.

-AMEN-

"SHE IS CLOTHED IN STRENGTH, DIGNITY, AND SHE LAUGHS WITHOUT FEAR OF THE FUTURE."

-PROVERBS 31:25-

-SPREAD YOUR WINGS-

DAY 10

GOALS

Create the Life you desire to live and always dreamed of. Each day set goals and try to work towards it. Setting goals is the first step in turning the invisible into the visible. Stay focus on the fulfillment of your goals instead of distractions.

SUCCESS NEVER HAPPENS ON ACCIDENT.

PLAN TO SUCCEED IN ALL THINGS.

GOAL: OUT DO THE OLD YOU!

YOU ARE A GOAL GETTER!!!

CHALLENGE WRITE DOWN YOUR GOALS AND EXECUTE YOUR GOALS.

AFFIRMATION:

I ACCEPT THE LIFE I DESERVE.

PRAYER

DEAR LORD,

I ENTER YOUR GATES WITH THANKSGIVING AND PRAISE. COVER ME, MY FAMILY AND FRIENDS.

-AMEN-

"THE PAIN THAT YOU'VE BEEN FEELING, CAN'T COMPARE TO THE JOY THAT'S COMING."

-ROMAN 8:18-

-SPREAD YOUR WINGS-

DAY 11

FOCUS

Focus is the center of interest or activity. This is easy at the beginning because you're focused on what you stand to gain from achieving your goal. As time goes on, you may gradually forget how excited you were and start to lose that inner fire. Remember to take things day by day. Nothing happens fast or overnight. Stay focus on what you believe in.

Stay focused on God & pray when you feel overwhelmed.

CHALLENGE Stay consistent and remember to take it day by day.

AFFIRMATION:

I WILL STAY FOCUS AND REMAIN FOCUS.

PRAYER

DEAR LORD,

I COME TO YOU HUMBLE AND THANKFUL. PLEASE GIVE ME THE STRENGTH TO PUSH THROUGH DAILY.

-AMEN-

FINALLY, BE STRONG IN THE LORD AND IN HIS MIGHTY POWER.

-EPHESIANS 6:10-

-SPREAD YOUR WINGS-

DAY 12

KNOW YOUR WORTH

Knowing your worth is the sense of one's own value or worth as a person, self-esteem and self-respect. Start believing in your true value as a woman. Deem yourself as worthy of being treated good and valuable. Knowing your worth means having confidence in yourself. Your self-esteem is high. There is so much power in a woman. A woman can carry and deliver. So, carry yourself well and deliver your presence as a well-respected woman. You're worthy of all good things.

There's something about a woman presence when she values herself. Her presence demands respect without her having to say anything. YOU ARE A DIAMOND. YOU DESERVE THE BEST.

CHALLENGE Know your WORTH and STOP giving people discounts.

AFFIRMATION:

I WILL ALWAYS WALK WITH MY HEAD HIGH.

PRAYER

DEAR LORD,

I WALK BY FAITH AND NOT BY SIGHT. THANK YOU FOR SHOWING ME THE WAY.

OPEN DOORS THAT NEED TO BE OPEN AND CLOSE DOORS THAT NEED TO BE CLOSED.

-AMEN-

"ASK, AND IT WILL BE GVEN TO YOU; SEEK, AND YOUWILL FIND; KNOCK, AND IT WILL BE OPENED TO YOU."

-MATTHEW 7:7-

-SPREAD YOUR WINGS-

DAY 13

FORGIVENESS

There is purpose in every painful experience you been through. Those who live in the past have a hard time moving forward. Make peace with the past and forgive yourself. We all have made some good decisions and some bad ones as well. Forgive those who hurt you. Forgiving with expectation is NOT really forgiving. When someone apologizes to you, you are expecting them not to do it again. Reality is they just may do it again. You have the control to forgive and not be in the same position of being HURT again.

You can't change people, but you can change how you deal with them. Hurt people hurt people. Forgive yourself, forgive them and move forward. Let no one have power over you to keep you from destiny.

CHALLENGE Do forgive but DON'T forget. Make peace and move on forward.

AFFIRMATION:

I FORGIVE MYSELF AND I APOLOGIZE TO MYSELF.

PRAYER

DEAR LORD,

FORGIVE ME FOR MY SINS AND FORGIVE MY ENEMIES. CREATE IN ME A CLEAN HEART.

-AMEN-

"A SOFT ANSWER TURNS AWAY WRATH,
BUT A HARSH WORD STIRS UP ANGER."

-PROVERBS 15:1-

-SPREAD YOUR WINGS-

DAY 14

HIGH EXPECTATIONS

Wake up every day with high expectations. When we expect more, we will begin to see more, and be more. Think outside your comfort zone. Sometimes we live in this small box of thinking. This small box can cause us not to see all that life has to offer.

God created this beautiful world for us to see different things.

Do something different than the normal.

CHALLENGE Spend time trying NEW things and NEW ways. Do it different for a different result.

AFFIRMATION:

I AM OPEN TO NEW THINGS.

PRAYER

DEAR LORD,

FORGIVE ME FOR YESTERDAY, THANK YOU FOR TODAY AND BLESS ME WITH TOMORROW.

-AMEN-

"THERE IS A TIME FOR EVERYTHING AND A REASON FOR EVERY ACTIVITY UNDER THE HEAVENS."

=ECCLESIASTES 3:1-

-SPREAD YOUR WINGS-

DAY 15

I speak healing over your mind, body and soul. Remember you are healed and made whole by his stripes. Think about a broken mirror. You can't fix a broken mirror, look in it and get the same reflection. Those broken pieces in you, only can be healed by time and by God.

Pray over your body for good health. Watch what you take in, physically and mentally. Create healthy habits for your life. Your mind, body and soul matter.

CHALLENGE Create healthy habits that are good for your mind, body and soul.

AFFIRMATION:

I AM HEALED AND MADE WHOLE.

PRAYER

DEAR LORD,

HEAL THE BROKEN PIECES IN MY HEART. RESTORE ME AND LET ME HEAR YOU AND NOTHING BUT YOU.

-AMEN-

"I WILL NOT CAUSE PAIN WITHOUT ALLOWING SOMETHING NEW TO BE BORN, SAYS THE LORD."

-ISAIAH 66:9-

-SPREAD YOUR WINGS-

DAY 16

BREAKTHROUGH

Stand for something or fall for anything. We can lose ourselves and go on this merry go round. This merry go round is called going through cycles. We are suppose to go through seasons and not cycles.

Self-check if you are experiencing cycles. Evaluate your situation and how you got to that point. The breakthrough is coming. Stand firm and stand strong.

CHALLENGE Don't breakdown BUT BREAKTHROUGH. YOU ARE DESTINED FOR GREATNESS.

AFFIRMATION:

I AM IN A SEASON OF BREAKTHROUGH.

PRAYER

DEAR LORD,

HELP ME TO BREAKTHROUGH EVERY CYCLE IN MY LIFE. CONTNUE TO SHINE LIGHT OVER ME IN JESUS NAME.

-AMEN-

HE SENT FROM ABOVE, HE TOOK ME, HE DREW ME OUT OF MANY WATERS.

-PSALMS 18:16-

-SPREAD YOUR WINGS-

DAY 17

SELF-DISCIPLINE

Self-discipline is the ability to control one's feeling and overcome one's weakness; the ability to pursue what one thinks is right despite temptations to abandon it.

It is important to stay grounded and have will power. Self-discipline gives you the power to stick to your decisions and follow them through. It is an essential life skill that many successful people have. You are worth the things you want and the things you want are worth the you.

CHALLENGE Do NOT give up despite failures and setbacks. Resist distractions and temptations.

AFFIRMATION:

I AM A WOMAN OF VICTORY.

PRAYER

DEAR LORD,

GIVE ME THE STRENGTH TO ENDURE. HELP ME TO FOCUS ON YOU AND NOT TEMPTATION.

-AMEN-

HE BROUGHT ME FORTH ALSO INTO A LARGE PLACE; HE DELIVERED ME, BECAUSE HE DELIGHTED IN ME.

-PSALMS 18:19-

-SPREAD YOUR WINGS-

DAY 18

SELF-CONFIDENCE

Confident women don't mirror others to find what makes them happy. Women of confidence are happy in their own skin. They don't try to fit in. Women with confidence don't believe in being average.

Be not conformed of the world. Be renewed and stand different.

You are unique. You are treasure in the presence of the Lord.

CHALLENGE Dress for Success. Think positive about yourself. Do something today that makes you smile. You are beautifully made. Shine bright like a diamond.

AFFIRMATION:

I AM A GOD'S MATERPIECE.

PRAYER

DEAR LORD,

I ASK THAT YOU BLESS MY HEART DESIRES AND I PRAY OVER EVERYONE IN NEED OF YOU.

-AMEN-

BUT I TRUSTED IN THEE, O LORD: I SAID, THOU ART MY GOD.

-PSALMS 31:14-

-SPREAD YOUR WINGS-

DAY 19

BE BOLD

Own your true feelings. Self-assured woman owns up to their feelings. Whether the feeling is right or wrong. Live in truth and accept truth. Be confident in your feelings. Sometimes we as women tend to push our feelings aside to comfort others. In the end you only feel unsatisfied.

Take the opportunity to express your feelings without blaming others, and confirm that you are understood. Be bold but kind. Be bold, beautiful and have bold faith.

CHALLENGE Let your presence Speak and Speak in your Presence.

AFFIRMATION:

I AM WISE AND BOLD.

PRAYER

DEAR LORD,

THANK YOU FOR TODAY. PLEASE CONTINUE TO GIVE ME WISDOM AND KNOWLEDGE.

-AMEN-

AND BY KNOWLEDGE SHALL THE CHAMBERS BE FILLED.

-PROVERBS 24:4-

-SPREAD YOUR WINGS-

DAY 20

WOMEN EMPOWER WOMEN

WHEN YOU ARE A SELF-ASSURED WOMAN, YOU HAVE NO PROBLEM RECOGNZING GREATNESS IN ANOTHER WOMAN.

In today's society, a lot of women bash other women. We see on reality television there is more hate and jealousy, than actual love giving. Women should keep other women encouraged. It could go a long way. You never know what that woman is battling with. Love watching the people around you soar and believe you will continue to soar as well. Worthy women know their worth and do not have time for drama. They're NOT caught up in mess all the time, not negative and they don't hang around those type of people.

Keep positivity around you and in you. Let go of all negative thoughts and people.

Carry yourself with respect and receive respect.

CHALLENGE Keep your friends and family encouraged. Continue to pray for them. Be kind and be true. Help someone in need today.

AFFIRMATION:

I AM A WOMAN OF EMPOWER.

PRAYER

DEAR LORD,

THANK YOU FOR LIGHT. THANK YOU FOR EVERYTHING I HAVE AND CONTINUE SHINING YOUR LIGHT ON ME.

-AMEN-

HE SHALL NOT MAKE HIMSELF UNCLEANFOR HIS FATHER, OR FOR HIS MOTHER, FOR HIS BROTHER, OR FOR HIS SISTER, WHEN THEY DIE: BECAUSE THE CONSECRATION OF HIS GOD IS UPON HIS HEAD.

-NUMBERS 6:7-

-SPREAD YOUR WINGS-

DAY 21

SELF-CARE

You are a worthy woman. Your self-care is a priority. Make time for the basics and reward yourself. Maintaining a confident attitude comes along with you taking care of yourself. Relaxation, quiet time, eating well and grooming helps you feel better. Maintain a healthy relationship with yourself and it will boost your self-esteem.

Practicing self-care help you prevent feeling burned out and overwhelm. Also, it helps reduce stress and help you refocus.

CHALLENGE Get dress, do your hair and go have some fun. Take your mind off all the serious things and live life. Make time for you to relax.

AFFIRMATION:

I WILL TAKE CARE OF MYSELF.

PRAYER

DEAR LORD,

THANK YOU FOR HELPING ME BREAK BAD HABITS. THANK YOU FOR CREATING ME IN YOUR IMAGE.

-AMEN-

*SO GOD CREATED MAN IN HIS OWN IMAGE,
IN THE IMAGE OF GOD CREATED HE HIM;
MALE AND FEMALE CREATED HE THEM.*

-GENESIS 1:27-

-SPREAD YOUR WINGS-

WORDS OF ENCOURAGEMENT FOR YOU

DISTANCE YOURSELF FROM PEOPLE THAT....

MISTREAT YOU, NEGATIVE, LIE TO YOU, PUT YOU DOWN, HAVE NO GOALS, ABUSIVE AND THAT BRING OUT THE WORST IN YOU.

HIS ATTENTION MEANS NOTHING IF HE DON'T RESPECT YOU.

DON'T EXPECT PEOPLE TO LOVE AND RESPECT YOU, IF YOU DON'T RESPECT AND LOVE YOURSELF.

TAKE PRIDE IN WHO YOU ARE AND IN WHAT YOU HAVE TO OFFER.

SURROUND YOURSELF WITH POSITIVE WHO PEOPLE DOING POSITIVE THINGS.

NEVER FORGET ABOUT YOU AND WHAT MAKES YOU HAPPY.

YOU ARE WORTHY OF HAPPINESS, JOY AND PEACE.

YOU ARE A WORTHY WOMAN!!

GOD LOVES YOU ALWAYS AND UNCONDITIONALLY!!!

GET BACK TO YOU

&

JORNAL YOUR THOUGHTS/GOALS

WRITE

YOU ARE A BUTTERFLY

SPREAD YOUR WINGS

&

FLY

Made in the USA
Lexington, KY
02 May 2018